Inside
AMERICAN POLITICS

Lobbyists

By Anita Croy

LUCENT

Published in 2019 by
Lucent Press, an Imprint of Greenhaven Publishing, LLC
353 3rd Avenue
Suite 255
New York, NY 10010

For Brown Bear Books Ltd
Editorial Director: Lindsey Lowe
Managing Editor: Tim Cooke
Designer: Lynne Lennon
Design Manager: Keith Davis
Picture Manager: Sophie Mortimer
Children's Publisher: Anne O'Daly

Picture Credits
Front cover: eurobanks/Shutterstock.com
Interior: iStock: Bboserup, 24, DNY59, 30, dszc, 35, Jet City Image, 25, tovia, 12; **Library of Congress:** 18, 19, 20; **Public Domain:** 21, AgnosticPreachersKid, 6, 45, Madeleine Ball, 31, J Crocker, 36, Frick Art Reference Library Photoarchive, 17, Jorge Royan, 14, Gage Skidmore, 23, Virginia Education, 8, U.S. Government, 32; **Shutterstock:** Tono Balaguer, 37, Heidi Besen, 41, clicksabhi, 44, M Cornelius, 33, Da-ga, 5, DavidNNP, 11, Chris Dorney, 38, Evan El-Amin, 22, EQRoy, 15, Everett Historical, 16, Joseph Gruber, 7, Kathy Hutchins, 27, Anne Kitzman, 42, KMH Photovideo, 39, Mark Reinstein, 28, 40, Craig Russell, 10, Rena Schild, 13, Joseph Sohm, 29, Sportmatick Ltd, 34, Underawesternsky, 43, Jonathan Weiss, 26, Woodys Photos, 4; courtesy of **St Paul Saints Baseball:** 9.

Brown Bear Books has made every attempt to contact the copyright holders.
If you have any information please contact licensing@brownbearbooks.co.uk

Cataloging-in-Publication Data

Names: Croy, Anita.
Title: Lobbyists / Anita Croy.
Description: New York : Lucent Press, 2019. | Series: Inside American politics | Includes glossary and index.
Identifiers: ISBN 9781534566620 (pbk.) | ISBN 9781534566637 (library bound) |
ISBN 9781534566644 (ebook)
Subjects: LCSH: Lobbying–United States–Juvenile literature. |
Pressure groups–United States–Juvenile literature.
Classification: LCC JK1118.C79 2019 | DDC 328.73'078–dc23

Printed in the United States of America

CPSIA compliance information: Batch #BW19KL: For further information contact Greenhaven Publishing LLC, New York, New York at 1-844-317-7404.

Please visit our website, www.greenhavenpublishing.com. For a free color catalog of all our high-quality books, call toll free 1-844-317-7404 or fax 1-844-317-7405.

Contents

Chapter 1

MAKING
A CASE

Most people have heard of lobbyists, but not many people know exactly what they do. A lobbyist's job is to try to influence people's decisions—particularly those of people in power, such as politicians. Imagine your school needs new sports equipment but the school budget has already been spent. What could you do? Your class could write to the school board explaining why you need the equipment now, not next year. That makes you lobbyists!

Whenever public bodies such as school boards have money to spend on items such as sports equipment, people have the right to try to influence their spending priorities.

At state and national levels, lobbying is a vital part of the political process. It is almost as old as the Constitution. The First Amendment to the Constitution guaranteed the right to free speech. That includes lobbying because, in its simplest form, lobbying is just talking to somebody to try to persuade them to adopt a particular way of thinking.

Show Us the Money!

Many people have a negative view of lobbyists. This is because lobbyists are paid for their work, and the most successful lobbyists earn a lot of money. They charge to represent their clients' interests in Washington, D.C. Lobbyists **liaise** between politicians and huge corporations, trade associations, labor unions, and even wealthy individuals. Many clients of lobbyists are **special interest groups**. One such group is the National Rifle Association (NRA), which promotes the

In 2017, the lobbying industry in the United States was worth more than $10 billion in lobbyists' fees and the benefits gained for clients.

right to bear arms. Almost any cause has some kind of lobbyist representing it in the nation's capital as well as at a local and state levels.

Many lobbyists have offices based on K Street in downtown Washington, D.C. Lobbyists include former politicians and staffers who understand how best to influence lawmakers.

What Does a Lobbyist Do?

Some people argue that lobbying is undemocratic because it gives unelected representatives too much power. Lobbyists are socially and professionally well-connected, so they can meet politicians at all levels of government to try to influence them. Lobbyists have been behind many new laws and changes to the law. Much of a lobbyist's work takes place over lunch or dinner or in boxes at football or baseball games. That makes their activities seem **unaccountable**. In fact, however, lobbying is strictly regulated.

— WHAT DO YOU THINK? —

Many lobbyists are former politicians. They are often friends with the lawmakers they seek to influence. Do you think they should be allowed to exploit their familiarity with the political system to help their clients? How could they be prevented from doing so?

THE POWER OF THE PEOPLE

The politics in the nation's capital, Washington, D.C., often seem far removed from people's daily lives. In fact, politics affects every aspect of life, and lobbying gives people far more power to change things than they might think. Signing an online **petition** is a form of lobbying. Writing to local politicians or attending demonstrations are more ways people can make their voices heard.

Politics on Capitol Hill can seem remote from the lives of ordinary people, but in many ways lobbyists act as intermediaries between elected officials and the people they represent.

Chapter 2

WHAT IS LOBBYING?

The US Constitution was ratified in 1788 and came into effect the following year. It created a contract between the American people and the government. However, a group of politicians known as the Anti-Federalists were concerned that it gave power to the government rather than to the citizens. They addressed this by proposing the Bill of Rights, which included 10 amendments to the Constitution. The bill became law on December 15, 1791.

The First Amendment

The First Amendment declares: "Congress shall make no law … prohibiting the free speech thereof; or abridging the freedom of speech, or of the press; or of the right of the people peaceably to assemble, and to petition the Government for a redress of grievances."

Politicians known as Anti-Federalists influenced the Bill of Rights to ensure that no individual had too much power.

One common way for lobbyists to gain access to politicians is to give them tickets to important sporting events, theater shows, or concerts.

The Constitution guarantees both the right to free speech and the right to petition the government. A petition is a formal request that a particular action should be taken. Lobbying is therefore protected as one of the ways in which the people can be represented in the government.

Who Lobbies?

Almost anyone can become a lobbyist or can employ professional lobbyists. The aim of lobbying is to represent a particular interest group. This sometimes contributes toward the negative view of lobbyists, by suggesting they favor the interests of the few over the many. Yet the interest groups represented by lobbyists are not exclusive.

Thanks to social media, you do not have to be a Washington lobbyist to launch a campaign for political change. Petition websites such as change.org work by offering subscribers a chance to vote for many different causes. Anyone can start a petition online. The more people who sign it, the more those in power will listen. In 2011, fourth graders used change.org to petition Universal Studios. The students wanted the studio to include an environmental message on the website for the Dr. Seuss movie *The Lorax*. The petition gathered 57,000 signatures and Universal changed the website to include messages about protecting trees.

Interest groups could include most Americans. Lobbyists represent the interests of schools and students, of the sick, of people from particular regions, or workers in particular industries. Gender, age, religion, or hobbies all put people within groups that might need political representation.

How Do Lobbyists Work?

Much of lobbying work is about who you know. It is vital to be able to have access to people who influence laws, because they are in a position to change things. Knowing lawmakers is essential. Many lobbyists are former politicians and Washington insiders. They understand how to get things done, and know many of the people who hold real power in the government. Face-to-face meetings are vital in the world of lobbying. Lobbyists often eat out three times a day so they can meet politicians or their staffers. They might take a politician or staffer to a sports event or concert. They might hold fundraisers to raise money for politicians.

Bars and restaurants in Washington, D.C., such as 1789 or the Blue Duck Tavern, are traditional locations for meetings between politicians and lobbyists.

WHAT DO YOU THINK?

Many people think that lobbying is another word for bribing or buying influence. Do you think it is possible for politicians to take money from lobbyists and remain **impartial**? In what ways do you think receiving money might change a politician's behavior?

The lobbyist does not pay for these activities. His or her clients provide the funding as part of their effort to persuade politicians to support their interests. Such interactions between lobbyists, their clients, and politicians are entirely legal.

Lobbying Rules

Critics of lobbying claim that clients with the biggest checkbooks get the most results. They say it allows wealthy corporations to "buy" lawmakers. In fact, lobbying is subject to strict rules. All states require lobbyists to report lobbying and to declare donations, gifts, or **hospitality** above a certain amount, which varies from state to state. In Washington, D.C., federal rules do not allow politicians to accept gifts totaling above $100 from lobbyists in any year.

Individual gifts from lobbyists to politicians can cost no more than $50, and only two gifts are allowed each year.

WHAT DO YOU THINK?

Should there be any limits on lobbyists' giving gifts to politicians? If there was unlimited spending, what might be the consequences? Would it matter, as long as everyone knew about it?

Ways of Lobbying

Political lobbyists traditionally work by building face-to-face relationships with the politicians they wish to influence. In the 2000s, however, new methods of influencing politicians emerged, thanks mainly to Facebook and other social media campaigns. Politicians find it difficult to ignore mass responses to events such as the Parkland, Florida, high school shooting in February 2018, in which 17 people were killed and 17 wounded. Such high-profile social media campaigns are a new form of lobbying that threatens to change the nature of political influence.

Marchers in Philadelphia call for increased solar power. Causes such as environmental change can attract mass support, even if they lack powerful lobbyists in Washington, D.C.

Chapter 3

LOBBYING IN HISTORY

Lobbying is as old as the United States itself, and has gone on throughout American history. The term "lobbying" originated in Great Britain. It dates back to the 1640s, when political deals were often made in the **lobbies** outside the main debating chambers of the Houses of Parliament in London. When the US Constitution was drafted in 1787, following US independence from Britain, the Anti-Federalists were determined that the new political system would not allow any interest group to have too much power. They argued that by ensuring different interest groups had a voice, the interests of everyone would be served democratically.

The lobby of the House of Commons in London has room for people to meet informally—unlike the cramped debating chamber.

An Old Practice

Ever since the first session of the US Congress in 1789, people have lobbied politicians. In the early years of the republic, a group of New York merchants deliberately delayed the passing of **tariff** bills by wining and dining Congressmen so that they missed crucial votes in Congress. Lobbying has often been closely connected with

The First Bank of the United States was built in Philadelphia in 1795.

business. Several board members of the first bank in the newly independent America, the Bank of the United States, were Congressmen. They were making the country's laws while at the same time being paid by the bank. Today, that would be seen as a conflict of interest that might influence their votes.

For much of the 1800s, most lobbying took place at a state level. It was only when the federal government took control of the economy and government became more centralized that lobbying moved to the capital in Washington, D.C.

In the capital, many lobbyists soon started to pretend to be members of the press in order to gain access to legislators in Congress. In 1879, new rules were introduced. These said that members of the press had to be registered in order to sit in the press galleries in the House or the Senate in order to guarantee that they were genuine.

Businesses and individuals lobbied for contracts to build railroads in the West. The government encouraged construction by giving away vast areas of land the railroad companies could sell off.

The Gilded Age

Between the end of the Civil War (1861–1865) and the end of the nineteenth century, the United States industrialized rapidly and expanded westward in what was called the Gilded Age. Expansion brought great opportunities for businessmen. During the presidency of Ulysses S. Grant, from 1869 to 1877, rich industrialists and emerging corporations controlled the country's political situation. The best example was the powerful railroad lobby.

Private investors were reluctant to risk investing in a transcontinental railroad, so the government gave out huge subsidies and land grants to railroad companies. In 1872, a scandal exposed **bribes** the Union Pacific Railroad had paid to Congressmen in order to secure government contracts. The bribes left Union Pacific heavily in debt and made a few politicians very rich.

King of the Lobby

One of the most successful lobbyists of the 1860s and 1870s was Samuel Cutler Ward. Ward came up with the idea that lobbying would be most effective if it was based on developing friendships. Known as an outstanding chef and a generous host, Ward entertained on a lavish scale in order to lobby for clients from insurance companies, mining companies, and steamship owners. For more than a decade, the well-connected Ward brought together politicians and businessmen at his social gatherings. Ward's social lobbying laid the foundations for the modern lobbying profession.

Samuel Cutler Ward, known as the King of the Lobby, with his wife, Emily Astor.

Reconstruction

Following the devastation caused by the Civil War, intense rebuilding

WHAT DO YOU THINK?

The kind of social lobbying invented by Samuel Cutler Ward is often criticized. Do you think people would trust lobbyists more if lobbying was separated from social activity? How might that change lobbying?

took place in the South. The government allocated money to state governments for this Reconstruction, and state legislatures in the South became the sites of intense lobbying as businesses competed for a share of the funds. Railroad constructors, for example, argued that one of the many reasons the South had been at a disadvantage during the Civil War was its lack of railroads. Meanwhile, the Louisiana State Lottery successfully lobbied the governor and the state legislature to approve its license to sell lottery tickets in New Orleans in 1866.

The Twentieth Century

During the Progressive Era, from the 1880s to the 1920s, lobbying attracted intense criticism. Many people worried that the corruption of the Grant presidency might continue. The criticism grew louder in 1928. It was discovered that the American Tariff League had hired two professional lobbyists to help elect Herbert Hoover as president. Many people began to demand that lobbying should become far more transparent.

The Mississippi Valley Railroad was built in 1882, during a period of intense building in the South.

Herbert Hoover (right) rides in an open car to his presidential inauguration, alongside outgoing president Calvin Coolidge.

It was only in 1953 that the Supreme Court set down a legal definition of lobbying. The Court declared that lobbying was any act seeking influence made directly to Congress, its members, or its committees. The Court distinguished lobbying from indirect lobbying, which is an attempt to influence Congress by changing public opinion on an issue.

Lobbying Takes Off

Lobbying moved to the heart of government during the 1970s, when raising money became key to campaign in elections. Then, in the 1990s, politicians began to use what were known as "congressional

> **WHAT DO YOU THINK?**
>
> Some lobbyists help politicians raise money to campaign in elections. How could elections be made cheaper, so that politicians do not have to rely on donors?

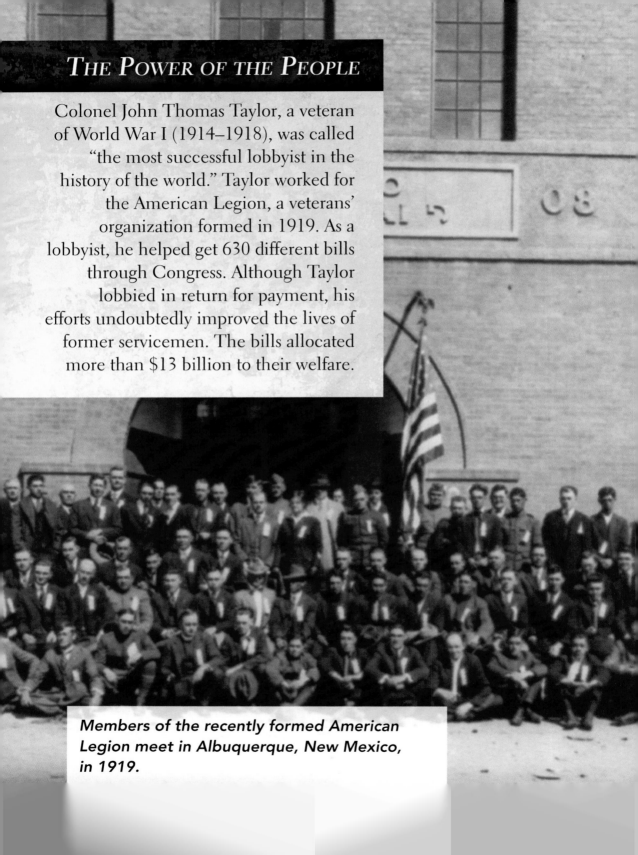

THE POWER OF THE PEOPLE

Colonel John Thomas Taylor, a veteran of World War I (1914–1918), was called "the most successful lobbyist in the history of the world." Taylor worked for the American Legion, a veterans' organization formed in 1919. As a lobbyist, he helped get 630 different bills through Congress. Although Taylor lobbied in return for payment, his efforts undoubtedly improved the lives of former servicemen. The bills allocated more than $13 billion to their welfare.

Members of the recently formed American Legion meet in Albuquerque, New Mexico, in 1919.

earmarks." Congressional earmarks were payments requested for certain purposes by politicians and often added to unrelated bills. They did not go through the usual oversight required for Congress to allocate funds. Lobbyists began to try to persuade politicians to make their clients **eligible** for these funds.

The Iraqi dictator Saddam Hussein was among Edward von Kloberg III's clients.

Defending the Indefensible

Lobbyist Edward von Kloberg III became infamous for a different reason. He lobbied in Washington, D.C., on behalf of some of the world's most despised dictators. Von Kloberg lobbied for anyone who paid him. He wanted Congress not to take sanctions against them. Von Kloberg argued that it was not his job to concern himself with his clients' reputations.

WHAT DO YOU THINK?

Do you think that lobbying for people or organizations with bad reputations should be allowed? What sort of people might be included on a banned list because of their activities?

Chapter 4

LOBBYING
TODAY

By the time President Barack Obama was sworn into office in January 2009, lobbying had evolved into a huge industry. It was unrecognizable from its origins just 30 years earlier.

Barack Obama was suspicious of lobbyists, but found it difficult to limit their influence.

Since the 1970s, government had grown more complicated. Critics said that it had become too large. New legislation had attempted to control the growing influence of lobbying, particularly the Lobbying Disclosure Act of 1995 and the Honest Leadership and Open Government Act of 2007. These acts defined a professional lobbyist as someone who is paid by a client, who has more than one lobbying "contact," and who spends 20 percent or more of their time on a single client during a three-month period. The new legislation soon had an effect. From a peak of 14,822 registered lobbyists in 2007, the number had fallen back to 12,655 by 2011.

What's in a name?

The definition of professional lobbyists in the acts is very narrow. It excludes many people who work as lobbyists who do not exactly fulfill the criteria. During the 2012 Republican primary campaign, for example, many people believed that the Speaker of the House, Newt Gingrich, was acting as a lobbyist by running a health-care consulting company. Clients paid the company a fee of $200,000 to represent their interests in the government. Gingrich insisted that he did not abuse his political position in order to further his clients' interests. By a strict interpretation of the law, he argued that he was not a lobbyist. His critics still believed, however, that he was.

Newt Gingrich founded the Center for Health Transformation in 2003. He claimed the organization promoted good medical practice, but his opponents said it was a lobby group.

President Obama limited lobbyists' access to the White House, but it had little effect on their influence on Capitol Hill.

The Obama Administration

Barack Obama was president from 2009 to 2017. He believed that lobbying had become too powerful in Washington, D.C., allowing some corporations to wield too much influence. He barred lobbyists from the White House. On his first full day in office, Obama signed an **executive order** that banned his appointees from lobbying their former colleagues for two years after they left

WHAT DO YOU THINK?

Do you think that certain lobbyists support causes that are more important than others? Why might lobbies that protect the environment be considered more important than lobbies concerned with protecting mining jobs?

government. This was to try to halt the so-called "revolving door" by which many former officials and their staff quit politics and instantly became lobbyists. Obama was not against all lobby groups. He encouraged voices that he felt were underrepresented, such as consumer rights groups and human rights groups. Environmental lobbyists were also welcomed.

Tackling the Corporations

President Obama's time in the White House coincided with the rise of some of the largest corporations that dominate modern American life, such as the online retailer Amazon. Such companies lobby fiercely to get the government to enact laws that will help them.

If national or state politicians use the "revolving door" to become lobbyists, they can increase their salaries by more than ten times.

By 2015, for example, Amazon was spending $9.4 million every year on lobbying. Amazon lobbied on all kinds of issues that were important to its business, from cyber security to welfare benefits for workers.

From 2010 onward, Amazon more than doubled its spending on lobbying the US government.

The White House tried to ban lobbyists working for corporations such as Boeing and General Electric from advisory committees, but the ban had no effect and was abandoned. In the same way, Obama's attempt to stop the revolving door also failed. A former White House press secretary, Jay Carney, became Amazon's Senior Vice President for Global Corporate Affairs. Loopholes in the legal definition of lobbyists allowed politicians and staffers to become lobbyists. Marilyn Tavenner, for example, was an official in the Department of Health and Human Services. She helped bring in Obama's reforms to the medical system, called Obamacare.

WHAT DO YOU THINK?

Do you think large corporations such as Amazon have too much influence? What advantages are there for corporations in becoming involved in national politics?

In 2015, the Hollywood actress and activist Gwyneth Paltrow lobbied Congress over the Safe and Accurate Food Labeling Act. She wanted to force companies to inform shoppers if food had been genetically modified. Two companies involved in genetically modified food, Monsant and Dupont, lobbied against the bill. Although the bill passed, it included a clause that said the label must only be readable by an app on a cell phone, making it far less informative for most shoppers.

High-profile celebrities such as Gwyneth Paltrow can be effective lobbyists because they attract press coverage and therefore raise public awareness about and support for particular issues.

However, Tavenner then became a leading lobbyist for the private health-insurance industry, which fought against Obamacare. Another example was Victoria Espinel, the leader of the software industry's lobbying group. As a member of the Obama administration, Espinel had headed up the negotiation and enforcement of intellectual property rules in the software industry.

"Drain the Swamp!"

During the presidential campaign of 2016, Donald Trump argued that Washington insider dealing, such as lobbying, was strangling the federal government. He said he would end the powerful lobbying industry as part of what he called "draining the swamp." On taking office, however, President Trump reversed Obama's ban on lobbyists in the White House. Trump encouraged industries he supports, such as the coal, steel, oil, and gas industries, to lobby Washington. In contrast, he made it harder for consumer or climate-change groups to gain access to White House officials.

During his presidential campaign, Donald Trump energized many voters distrustful of US politics with slogans such as "Drain the Swamp."

In contrast to President Obama, President Trump welcomed lobbying from industries he saw as being vital to the US economy, such as coal mining.

Trump also stopped the public disclosure of the daily logs that record who goes into the White House. This makes it harder for the public to find out who may be in a position to lobby the president and his officials. Some critics observe that this makes the process of government less transparent. Despite the president's campaign promises, lobbying costs continued to grow. In the first nine months of 2017, some $2.43 billion was spent on lobbying—a raise on the comparable figure from 2016, when $2.38 billion was spent.

WHAT DO YOU THINK?

Although President Trump promised to cut the influence of lobbyists, he did not do so.
Why is it more difficult to reduce the influence of lobbyists than it might appear?

Chapter 5

CONTROVERSIES
AND DEBATES

The history of lobbying is one of scandals and controversies. A long series of revelations has reinforced many people's opinion that lobbying should not be part of the political system. Other people argue that, without lobbying to keep them familiar with all the issues, politicians would not be able to do their jobs effectively.

The revolving door is so common that more than half of former senators now become lobbyists.

The Revolving Door

One of the scandals that creates most distrust is the revolving door. President Obama tried to stop the practice, saying it was a clear conflict of interest. To many other observers, the process is one in which politicians legally make use of contacts made while in public service to start a new career for themselves.

The Democrat Richard Gephardt, for example, was the House Majority leader in the early 1990s. When he stopped being a politician, he built a very lucrative business as a lobbyist. His clients included the Republic of Turkey, which some observers criticized as not being a true democracy.

Illegal Lobbying

One notorious lobbying scandal of the 2000s involved the lobbyist Jack Abramoff. Abramoff charged Native American tribes around $85 million dollars in return for lobbying the government to help the tribes gain gambling rights on reservation land. However, Abramoff pocketed around $45 million for himself. When the scandal was exposed in 2005, Abramoff was tried, found guilty, and sent to jail.

In an earlier scandal in 1989, five senators lobbied for generous banking concessions for the Lincoln Savings and Loans Association. The association was headed by Charles Keating who, in turn, contributed to the senators' campaign funds. When the bank collapsed owing $3 billion, Keating was sent to jail and the "Keating Five" were reprimanded for their actions.

Nicknamed "Casino Jack," Jack Abramoff served 43 months in jail and later wrote a book exposing Washington corruption.

Money, Money, Money

Critics of lobbying point out that, when large sums of money are involved, it is impossible to expect politicians to behave impartially. In part, the appeal of lobbying lies in the fact that politicians have more need of financial support than they did in the past. Over the last few decades, it has becoming increasingly expensive to run a campaign for any kind of political office in the United States.

In 2016, Speaker Paul Ryan spent $12 million on his campaign to be reelected to his seat in the House of Representatives.

WHAT DO YOU THINK?

Some people believe that campaign donations leave a candidate in debt to his or her donors. Should fundraising for electoral campaigns be banned? What other ways could be used to pay for elections?

THE POWER OF THE PEOPLE

In 2005, lobbyists for Ketchikan, Alaska, persuaded Alaskan politicians in Congress to support the building of a bridge from Ketchikan (population 9,000) to its Gravina island airport. The politicians included $220 million in a National Appropriations bill to build the Gravina Island bridge. The project was soon named "the bridge to nowhere." It became notorious after the Alaskan politicians refused to allow the funds to be diverted to hurricane relief in Louisiana. Public outrage forced Congress to abandon the bridge in 2007 and redistribute the funds where they would benefit more people.

Many Alaskans were among those who objected to the earmarking of a huge sum of federal money to benefit a relatively tiny number of people in the state.

33

The Cost of Campaigning

In 1976, it cost $86,000 to run a campaign for the House of Representatives. By 2017, the price had gone up to $1.5 million. Over the same period, the cost of winning a seat in the Senate rose from $609,000 to $8.8 million. That means that most politicians need to raise funds. Some of the funds are raised by campaigns,

Lobbyists work on behalf of candidates who are limited in what funds they can legally solicit.

but more are raised by political action committees (PACs) or super PACs. These provide indirect support for a candidate's campaign, such as screening TV ads criticizing their political opponents.

Lobbyists spend much of their time fundraising for prospective candidates or their PACs. In turn, candidates have come to rely on lobbyists as a crucial source of income. This gives lobbyists a great deal of potential influence over a politician's agenda.

WHAT DO YOU THINK?

PACs and super PACs do not have to reveal the identities of their funders. Do you think voters should be told who pays for election campaigns? How might that influence voting choices?

Disclosing Lobbying

The Lobbying Disclosure Act of 1995 failed to achieve transparency in the lobbying of the federal government. If he or she fails to register, a lobbyist can face a fine of up to $50,000. However, lobbyists can make far greater sums, so it is worth their while risking getting caught in order to operate free of legal restriction. In addition, it is easy to find ways around registering. Lobbyists just need to state that they do not spend more than 20 percent of their time on any one client, and they have no need to register. State fees and fines for lobbyists are also easily affordable. Critics of the lobbying system believe that the fees charged are too low and that there are too many loopholes that allow some lobbyists to avoid official registers.

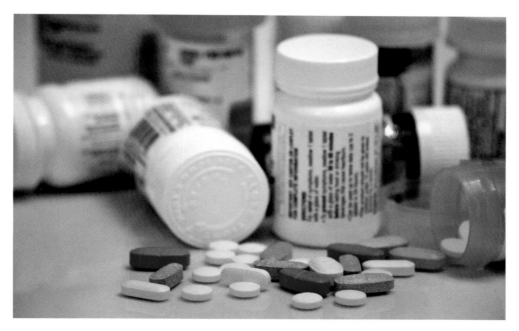

The pharmaceuticals industry is one of the biggest spenders on US political lobbying, which was worth a total of $3.15 billion in 2016.

Chapter 6

LOBBYISTS AND YOU

Lobbying is not just a remote activity that goes on in Washington, D.C. It works on a state and local level, too, and it affects everyone. Whether they are passed in Washington or in the state capital, most laws impact our lives in some way. Almost every bill that passes has been changed by politicians in the legislature. Sometimes those changes are in the public interest—but at other times they have been suggested by interest groups to help their own interests rather than those of the public.

Lobbyists often work in big buildings in busy cities.

The Biggest Lobbyist

The biggest lobbying spender in the country in 2015 was the US Chamber of Commerce. This is a nongovernment association that represents its members, consisting of more than three million US businesses of varying sizes.

The lobbying expenses of the Chamber of Commerce were more than 2.5 times higher than the next highest spender in the same year, the American Medical Association. With its member firms working on a local, state, and national level, the Chamber of Commerce broadly supports the Republican Party. It is also part of the revolving door. In 2018, 78 of its 166 lobbyists previously held government positions.

The Chamber of Commerce and You

Lobbyists working for the Chamber of Commerce have an influence on everyone's lives. While their job is to promote the specific interests of their members, the lobbyists also work to promote business interests at every level. Since 2000, for example, they have helped to defeat several attempts to pass climate change legislation. They have also lobbied against antitobacco policies in other countries.

The first Chamber of Commerce in North America was started by New York merchants in 1768 to lobby for their business interests.

In 2009, Chamber of Commerce lobbyists opposed President Obama's Affordable Health Care for America Act.

The Gun Lobby

One of the most controversial lobby groups is the National Rifle Association (NRA). It represents fewer than one-fifth of the nation's gun owners, but it is the

Organizations such as the NRA have a high public profile, which benefits their lobbying efforts.

most powerful gun lobby in the country. It has successfully blocked new gun legislation following mass shootings in the last decade, such as the Parkland, Florida, high school shooting in February 2018. Critics argue that the NRA has disproportionate power because more than half the members of Congress have received either money or help from the NRA. Eight lawmakers have taken more than $1 million from the NRA, including the Florida Republican Senator Marco Rubio. Without the financial support of the

WHAT DO YOU THINK?

Defense companies gain most of their income from government contracts. They are active lobbyists in Washington, D.C. Should national defense be influenced by commercial considerations?

THE POWER OF THE PEOPLE

Following the Parkland shootings in Florida in February 2018, eleventh grader Cameron Kasky and four friends started the #NeverAgain movement on Twitter. Although the students were too young to vote, they led a new movement to change gun laws. They organized a March For Our Lives in Washington, D.C., on March 24, 2018. The march was joined by a further 800 marches across the nation involving hundreds of thousands of people. Their lobbying soon had an effect. Delta Airlines and Hertz both dropped their association with the NRA.

A large crowd made up mainly of students and other young people gather in the Florida state capital, Tallahassee, in February 2018 to call for increased gun control.

NRA, critics argue, it would be hard for some politicians to stay in office. The NRA spends little on lobbying in comparison with the pharmaceutical, tobacco, and insurance industries. However, it does spend far more than any of the groups lobbying for more gun control. In 2017, the NRA spent more than $10 million on lobbying. The highest-spending gun control lobby spent less than a fifth of that amount. This imbalance causes frustration in people who want to see the gun laws revised. Following the Parkland shootings, a new antigun lobby emerged, spearheaded by students.

The pro-life lobby is well represented in Washington, D.C. It is balanced by a high-profile lobby for women's rights.

Health Care and Insurance

The health care industry is one of the most powerful lobbying groups. Although many Americans agree that the health-care system must be improved, it has been very hard to pass legislation to reform the system. This partly reflects the influence of lobbyists protecting the interests of health care businesses. In 1993, the administration of President Bill Clinton tried to provide universal health care for Americans, but lobbying from insurance companies defeated the bill.

In 2010, President Obama signed the Patient Protection and Affordable Care Act (nicknamed Obamacare). It set out to ensure that all Americans had access to affordable health insurance. Since then, insurance companies have lobbied to get the bill repealed. President Trump came to office in 2017 committed to overturning the legislation.

Some Americans believe that health insurance firms use lobbying to effectively limit any meaningful debate on health care reform.

WHAT DO YOU THINK?

One defense of the lobbying system is that it represents everyone, because everyone belongs to at least one special interest group. What special interest groups do you think you might be part of?

Chapter 7

GETTING
INVOLVED

Lobbying has played a key role in US politics since the Anti-Federalists and the First Amendment. The right to free speech and the right to petition are protected by US law. However, lobbying has become inextricably linked to big money and the way politicians are elected. For many people, this makes lobbying an unwelcome

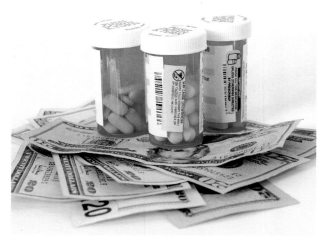

The large sums of money involved are one reason most Americans are suspicious of lobbying.

part of American politics. In a 2013 poll, only 6 percent of Americans believed that lobbyists were honest and ethical.

A Force for Good?

At its best, however, lobbying provides a supply of expertise. Effective lobbyists make sure legislators know the key facts on any given subject. They believe legislators will come to the right conclusions if they have the right information. Lobbying does not only work for business interests.

THE POWER OF THE PEOPLE

Social media has helped to transform popular lobbying. From petition sites such as change.org to Facebook and Twitter, it has never been easier to publicize an issue and gain support to put pressure on politicians to act. If you feel strongly about the lack of sports facilities in your local park, why not start your own petition? Or, if you want to see more gun control or more aid for refugees, for example, you could join a movement that has a strong lobbying voice.

If you want to change the opening hours of your local library, you can use social media or online petitions to gather enough support to make your case difficult to ignore.

In response to lobbying, Congress gave $25 million to support the poorest children around the world. The United States is the single largest donor to international child welfare.

Lobbying can also raise public awareness of causes such as poverty and slavery. The Child Survival Fund, for example, lobbied Congress in the 1980s for funds to help children's health and nutrition. Twenty-five years later, the number of under-five-year-olds dying each day around the world had reduced by half from 41,000 a day to 20,880.

Become a Lobbyist

In the same way that lobbying does not have to be associated with big business, neither does it have to be carried out by the large firms of K Street. Anyone can lobby an elected representative. If you have an issue, you can write to officials for your area. If there is something you feel particularly strongly about, get your friends to write, too.

Elected politicians have a duty to listen to the concerns of the people who vote for them. There are also ways you can influence professional lobbyists. If you belong to organized groups, such as the Scouts, they likely have lobbyists who look after their interests. Make sure your views are known on any debates within the organization.

Good or Evil?

Some people see lobbyists as a way to ensure that politicians are informed on issues. Others, however, see lobbying as an exercise in greed. One thing is for sure: lobbying works. One estimate says that, for every dollar it spends on lobbying, a corporation receives $220 in tax breaks. With such figures, lobbying looks set to stay at the heart of politics.

For many people, the expensive offices of K Street are a sign that lobbyists put money at the heart of American politics.

WHAT DO YOU THINK?

Lobbyists are very unpopular. Do you think the political system would be better off without them? Without lobbyists, what other ways could be used to channel information to lawmakers?

Glossary

bribes: money or gifts used to dishonestly persuade people to take a particular action

eligible: satisfying the conditions to qualify for something

executive order: a statement issued by the president that has the force of a law

hospitality: the entertainment of clients or official visitors

impartial: treating all rivals equally

liaise: to act as a link between different groups

lobbies: rooms such as hallways or entrances where people can meet

petition: a formal written request for official action, usually signed by a large number of people

special interest groups: groups of people or organizations that receive benefits through political lobbying

tariff: a tax or duty paid on particular types of imports or exports

unaccountable: describes someone who does not have to justify their actions or take responsibility for them

For More Information

Books

Donovan, Sandy. *Special Interests: From Lobbying to Campaign Funding.* Inside Elections. Minneapolis, MN: Lerner Publications, 2015.

Herschbach, Elisabeth. *Lobbyists and Special Interest Groups.* American Politics Today. Pittsburgh, PA: Eldorado Ink, 2016.

Rushford, Greg (ed.). *How Washington Actually Works for Dummies.* Hoboken, NJ: John Wiley & Sons, 2012.

Websites

Open Secrets
https://www.opensecrets.org/lobby/
A table of the increase in lobbying spending in the last 20 years.

Lobby It
http://lobbyit.com/resources/
An insiders' guide to lobbying by Washington lobbyists.

How Stuff Works
https://people.howstuffworks.com/lobbying.htm
A guide to how lobbying influences government.

Index